This book belong

First published in 2024 by KDP

ISBN: 9798339828211

Thank You, Nursery.

Joe Clapson

Saying goodbye to our babies is a
hard thing to do.

But you
made it easy
because they love seeing
you.

They don't look back when
they run through the door.

And they forget to say goodbye because they just want more...

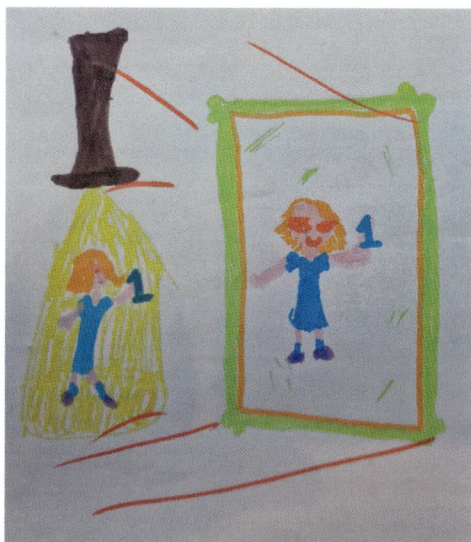

... Time at Nursery, time with all staff, time to play, and time to laugh.

From banging rolling pins with Mimi and friends in the Under-3s,

To laughing with both Marias with shakers made from peas.

Perry the in-house artist is always in demand, any character wished for, is scribbled on command.

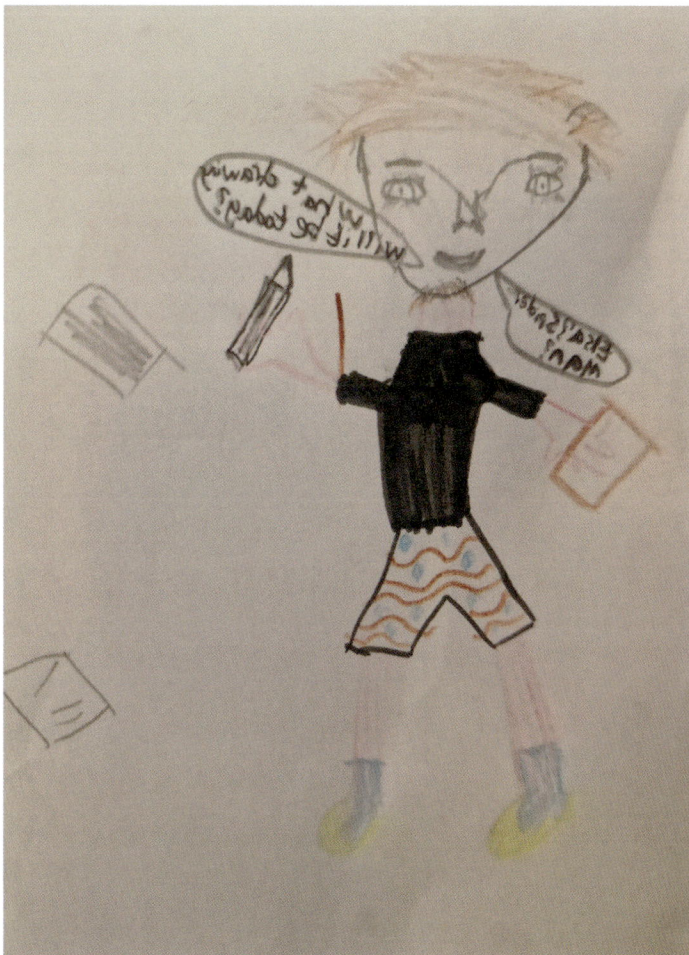

Georgina, what can we say, your energy and smile, brings happiness to everyone...

And you do it with such style.

The chant of "Baking, baking, baking!" will forever be in our minds.

Just like how you teach the power of always being kind.

A warm hug from Ana makes any child feel safe.

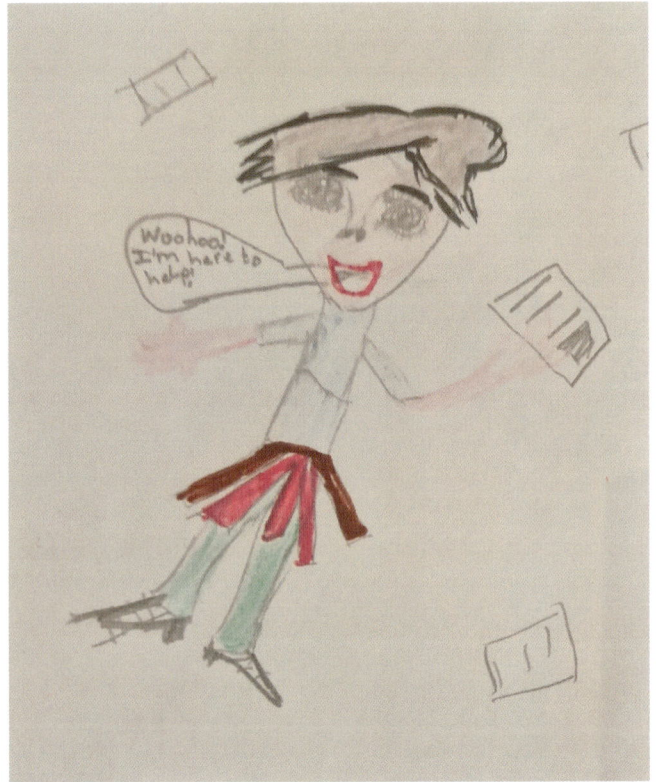

Her calm cuddles bring smiles to every single face.

Stepping up to Pre-school could be scary for kids, mums and dads.

But not for long at Willows,

With so much fun to be had.

The children's entertainer who goes by the name of Chris, has too many talents to even attempt to list.

Exploding bottles, phonics puppets, amazing fancy dress.

Story scripts and shows on stage – he's a hero, it must be stressed.

Magda, Sentheran, Sade,
you teach so many things.

From clay models and
dancing to seasonal songs
to sing.

Savita and Merlinda, you
have that special way,

of making little ones feel
special, each and every
day.

The celebrities at Willows are named Jim and Ted. Every child loves those guys, it really must be said.

"The best driver" and "the best at building stuff" –
5 star reviews are really not enough.

Willows nursery is so busy, with so much to get done.

And at the heart of everything is so much love and fun!

How it all happens is impossible to conceive.

But the brains behind the magic is the wonderful Genevieve!

We thank you so much

It cannot be overstated

Like nowhere else

Love-filled, it cannot be debated

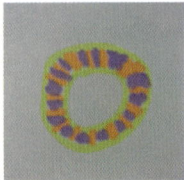

Outstanding staff, beyond compare

Wow!

Shine on, making memories for all the kids to share

Printed in Great Britain
by Amazon